Building Your Financial Ark

BUILDING
— YOUR FINANCIAL —
ARK

How to Survive & Thrive During the Next Economic Storm

Rockwall, Texas

Building Your Financial Ark: How to Survive and Thrive During the Next Economic Storm

Copyright ©2024 DPI Media, LLC

All Rights Reserved. No part of this publication may be reproduced, stored in a retrieval system, or transmitted, in any form or by any means, electronic, mechanical, photocopying, recording, or otherwise, without the prior written permission of the copyright holder. Printed in the United States of America.

For information, address David Phelps International LLC, 519 E. IH 30 Suite 246, Rockwall, TX 75087

Cover Design by Monica Austin, Mocah Studios, LLC
Interior Design by Imagine!® Studios, www.ArtsImagine.com

Cartoons licensed by www.CartoonStock.com. Used with Permission.

ISBN: 979-8-9860396-6-4 (paperback)
ISBN: 979-8-9860396-7-1 (e-book)

Library of Congress Control Number: 2024947295

First printing: October 2024

TABLE OF CONTENTS

Introduction . . . . *xi*
    How to Use This Book . . . . *xi*
    The Metaphor . . . . *xii*
    Why I Wrote This Book . . . . *xiii*

CHAPTER ONE
Taking the Helm of Your Financial Future 1

    Achieving and Maintaining Financial Autonomy
        in an Unfree World 1
    Getting Off the Hamster Wheel 5

CHAPTER TWO
Building Your Economic Hurricane Survival Plan 9

    Economic Storm Preparation Checklist 10
    Lessons in Wealth Preservation and Freedom
        from the World's Wealthiest Families 18

CHAPTER THREE
How to De-risk Your Portfolio 21

    Moving to Higher Ground 22
    Securing Wealth with Real, Tangible Assets 24
    DIY vs Strategic Collaboration—the Pathway to
        Passive Investing 28

CHAPTER FOUR
How to Conduct Due Diligence Amidst Market Upheaval 31

Due Diligence—Vetting the "Who" and the
   "How" of Prospective Investments. 34
The Importance of Aligning Incentives 38
Resisting the Siren Call of Big Returns 40
My "Under the Hood" Checklist for Any
   Investment 42
Becoming Your Own Financial Advocate 43

CHAPTER FIVE
How to Position for Opportunities from Chaos 47

Are You Ready for the Coming Opportunities? . . . 49

CHAPTER SIX
This Time IS Different . . . Secular Cycles and the Coming Economic Tsunami 51

The Rise in Interest Rates Will Affect All Equities
   and Commodities 52
The Risk of Recency Bias in Determining Future
   Strategy 55
The Uncertainty of "How Much Is Enough" in a
   Fast-Changing World. 57
What This Means for You 58

Table of Contents

CHAPTER SEVEN
Building a Legacy—an Ark to Preserve Freedom for the Next Generation 61

    Wealth Creation: The Foundation of Legacy 63
    Wealth Protection: Building a Fortress Around
        Your Legacy 66
    The Story of Joe Robbie: A Cautionary Tale 68
    Wealth Preservation: The Stewardship of Legacy . 70
    A Legacy Built on Stewardship 72

Conclusion: It Can't Happen Here—Wealth Intimidation and Loss of Autonomy 73
    Defending Your Freedom and Preparing for an
        Uncertain Future 77
    Becoming Your Own Financial Advocate 85
    The Fastest Path to Freedom and Autonomy 87
    This Economy Will Fall. Will You Fall with It? ... 88
    No Room for Error—Final Warning 88

Afterword: What Is Freedom Founders? 91

About the Author: Dr. David Phelps 99

To my fellow ark-builders:
The Freedom Founders tribe, composed of my amazing team, our courageous members, and our dedicated service providers, who continually show me that the best way to build an ark is to never do it alone.

INTRODUCTION

How to Use This Book

My name is Dr. David Phelps, and I am a contrarian by nature. To that end, not only will the content of this book be anti-traditional, but the layout of this book will also be a departure from conventional norms.

Most books begin by building out their backstory and philosophy for chapters and chapters, and THEN at the very end they MAY give you some practical advice on how to actually use what they're talking about.

This isn't one of those books.

In "Building Your Financial Ark", I am going to give you the practical action items in the beginning chapters. If you've picked up this book, chances are you and I have a lot in common. You are looking to protect yourself from economic upheaval. Whatever the reason, you don't need to be sold on the merits of moving to higher ground.

At the end of the book, I do include some chapters with a macro perspective of where we are in the market cycle, and what we can expect in the future. I also dig deeper into fundamentals, economics, and principles that provide the backbone for the action steps.

The Metaphor

This book's title is based on the Biblical story of Noah building an ark at God's direction to preserve his family during a worldwide flood. When the flood came, Noah and his family were safe—saved by the Ark.

It took Noah and his family many, many years to build the Ark, and during that time most people thought they were crazy. After all: Who would build a boat when there's no imminent prediction of rain?

The answer: Someone who knew a storm was coming.

Today, I believe there is a massive economic, social and political storm brewing. We are entering an era of change. The old models for success and security can no longer be relied upon to create the life we desire. Those who survive and thrive in the years ahead will need a different model.

As with Noah, my desire for building an ark (and teaching others to do the same) goes far beyond self-preservation. While Noah himself was safe in the Ark, the deeper purpose was the preservation of his children and the generations to come. It enabled future life to flourish on the earth.

The storm that is just beginning to land in our day will impact the next generation greatly. Make no mistake: the next generation is in for difficult challenges across the board. And unfortunately, school and peer groups often provide little in the way of real-world preparation. They are not taught fundamental financial acumen and life skills—in fact, many times they are taught the opposite.

That's where you and I come in.

Introduction

My hope is that through building your ark, you will be able to create a solid foundation that your children and grandchildren, and their children and grandchildren, will be able to build on to flourish in the decades to come.

There will be many who disagree. I wish them luck. No one has a crystal ball or can fully know the future. But when the storm breaks, it will be too late to build your ark.

The time to prepare is now.

Why I Wrote This Book

Not long ago, I was knee-deep in the day-to-day operations of my dental practice with the weight of the world on my shoulders. Wearing many "hats," I was a successful clinician blessed with good intellect and a strong work ethic. I was pursuing the American dream and had the perfect family, the perfect professional career and the perfect life.

But everything changed in the blink of an eye.

I suddenly found myself sitting beside my daughter's hospital bed. What followed was a multi-year battle with Leukemia and subsequent end-stage liver failure from the vicious rounds of chemotherapy that fought to save her life.

I'll never forget the long night after her six-hour liver transplant surgery. Sitting on a hard vinyl hospital bench, I finally came to terms with the reality that this was my wakeup call. I had no idea how much more time we would be given together.

> **Time and health were precious commodities that money couldn't buy.**

In that hospital room, I made a decision that would alter the course of my life. I decided to sell my dental practice and buy back my time.

Fortunately, I had spent the first 15 years of my practice career quietly building a financial "Ark" outside of my practice: A portfolio of single-family real estate where my funds were not locked up in a conventional, 401(k) retirement model. These were alternative investments that allowed me to access and control my hard-earned savings.

> **My Plan B "Ark" of alternative investments provided a clear path to buy back time before some distant, unknown retirement age. Without it, I could not have exited my practice in my early 40s.**

I still remember sketching out the numbers on the back of scraps of paper in that hospital room.
Did I have enough to make this "ark" work?

Introduction

The answer became clear. I wasn't some ultra-wealthy real estate tycoon. *But I had enough.* My ark was there when I needed it.

This decision wasn't easy, but it was necessary. My daughter's health crisis acted as a catalyst, pushing me towards this Plan B ark—investments that provided the passive income necessary to step away from dentistry and focus on what truly mattered: family, health, and freedom.

Fortunately, the alternate path that I took enabled me to build the cash flow streams needed to buy back my time when I needed it most. I had prepared, and my ark was ready when the storm hit.

I believe we are all about to face an even bigger storm. Economic winds have shifted and we are entering uncharted territory. This book is designed to give you clarity and help you chart a course for building your own ark—to provide you and your family with the stability, choices, and options you desire.

Fast forward 20 years, Jenna is doing great. By God's grace and the life-saving gift of a donor's liver, she is living a great life and pursuing her dreams. My girl is a fighter.

Today, I get to pursue what's most meaningful to me, too. In the years since selling my practice, I have come to discover that I was truly an entrepreneur disguised as a dentist. I have been given the space and permission to pursue my "Next"—helping colleagues learn the investment models that were so essential to my own freedom. I get to help them build their own arks and pursue what's most important to them.

It is more fulfilling and inspiring than anything I have ever done.

As my mentor Dan S. Kennedy often says . . . nothing is as good or as bad as it first appears.

> **"Nothing is as good or as bad as it first appears."**
>
> **—Dan S. Kennedy**

I am not a pessimistic person by nature. There will always be hard times both personally and in the broader economic cycles. But the hard times do not last forever. There will be light at the end of the tunnel. Preparation and prudence are necessary.

Those with resilience and faith will conquer and carry the torch forward.

It is in that belief that I write this book, and invite you to join me in preparing to prosper no matter what the future holds.

To your Freedom,

Dr. David Phelps, DDS

CHAPTER ONE

Taking the Helm of Your Financial Future

Achieving and Maintaining Financial Autonomy in an Unfree World

For practitioners who are ready to build a financial ark to sustain themselves and their families, the first responsibility is this: You must learn how to be the financial captain of your ship.

No one cares about your financial well being as much as you do. You can't rely on financial advisors (many of whom haven't lived through a storm like we're about to enter) or anyone else to be the captain for you.

Being your own captain means you make the ultimate decisions on how and where to invest. You are responsible for building your defensive and offensive positions, and navigating the economic tides.

Let me be clear: this takes work. You don't just jump into making investment decisions worth hundreds of thousands of dollars in a day.

But as a practitioner, you intrinsically understand the value of education. You invested heavily in yourself for many years of school, to develop the skill sets that now allow you to earn a higher than average income. It takes a similar degree of self-investment to develop the skill sets of investing and passive income creation.

As a practice professional or business owner, it's very difficult to find time to learn how investing and finance works. I get it. But I believe learning how to make your capital work for you is as critical, if not moreso, than learning how to make money in your career.

Most professionals and business owners fall short in this self-education for one of three reasons: Lack of time, lack of resources, or lack of support from their peers and society.

Society tells us implicitly not to learn investment skills. "*Just put your money in retirement vehicles and tax defer it. Give your money to a broker or advisor, and let them handle it.*"

Traditional financial planning is a badly flawed process. Most retirement plans will fail to reach their client's goals. Why? The industry focuses most of its effort chasing increasing net worth accumulation, and little time on the key to financial security—managing for cash flow.

Depleting the principal of one's retirement account over time leads to a scarcity mode of living, at a time when one should be able to enjoy the fruits of a long and successful career. Additionally, we enjoy a time when people are living longer with greater health than the previous generation. Such longevity requires retirement assets to last longer to offset the higher costs of inflation. Traditional plans don't provide this durability. The key to financial freedom is replacement income produced by owned assets.

> **The key to financial freedom is replacement income produced by owned assets.**

This accumulation model is the default. But the default best serves Wall Street and the employees who sell their products—who make their money regardless of whether your investments are going up or down.

You, on the other hand, have to hang on for dear life. It's thrilling when the market roller coaster is going up, but when the markets plummet—it makes your stomach churn.

Many years ago, before I became a dentist, I began studying how to be a better steward of my money. I studied books on investing in the stock market, mutual funds, and other Wall Street investments, and I also read books on real estate and tangible assets.

Tangible assets like real estate were the most attractive investments to me because of the direct control of their success. That's why we go into business (another tangible asset) in the first place: We want our hands directly tied to its success. We want to be able to control our own destiny and benefit from the superior effort, skill and sacrifice we are willing to put forth. We want to be a part of the equity, and are willing to put in the work to achieve it.

Those of us in business instinctively understand this opportunity. However, few extend the same philosophy to stewarding the proceeds of our success.

Why do hardworking professionals who run successful businesses hand their money over to others, to invest in products they don't understand?

Perhaps because they've been taught to do just that. Taught to believe that's what you're "supposed" to do. After all, this is what society conditions us for from the earliest ages. It is a narrative that is taught to us in school, and by well-meaning parents, mentors and peers.

But do other pathways exist? What are the alternatives?

Getting Off the Hamster Wheel

I've spoken with hundreds of hardworking doctors and their spouses through my work over the last 14 years. These doctors have provided very well for their families over the course of their careers. They've put their kids through good schools, lived in great neighborhoods, and accumulated all kinds of societal accolades. But few stop to reflect on how fragile this "success" really is. As long as your lifestyle is dependent on your ability to trade time for dollars, you are only one injury or unexpected life event away from financial disaster. Without alternative streams of income and a financial "Plan B", you are vulnerable to economic upheaval and have limited ability to adapt. You are not financially free.

> **As long as your lifestyle is dependent on your ability to trade time for dollars, you are only one injury or unexpected life event away from financial disaster.**

Many reach the latter half of their career only to wonder, "Where did all the money go?"

This leads to financial uncertainty and a gnawing sense that they are missing some key pieces to the puzzle of their future, and fear for what might happen in the event of a major correction or a destabilizing economic situation.

This uncertainty forces them to stay on the hamster wheel far longer than necessary. Most doctors cannot get off the hamster wheel because they don't have a suitable model or the proper blueprint/viable plan. They have abdicated their responsibility to financial advisors and products sold by someone "talking their book."

Randomized investing (a "spaghetti on the wall" approach) is very common for doctors and high-income professionals. Putting money here and there, wherever looks good at the time.

Most just plug and play like whack-a-mole. There's no coordination. No plan. No progress towards something that would actually replace their active income at a defined point in the future.

Without assets that produce cash flow to replace your income, you will always have to produce more yourself. For most, the scariest, most anxiety-inducing moment is leaving active income and doubting whether you have enough.

> **Without assets that produce cash flow to replace your income, you will always have to produce more yourself.**

That question of "How much money is enough?" is precisely what we help answer in Freedom Founders. The financial world can never provide an exact timeline or finish line for retirement, let alone mile markers to finally "having enough". This is because all their calculations are based on the accumulation model, where you can, at best, only predict a likelihood of outcomes.

With a cash flow model that is based on real, tangible assets vs Wall Street paper, you can determine with specificity when you have replaced your active income.

This allows you to start making decisions based on what matters most to you and not based on fear or worry.

This mindset shift is life changing. It is the key to translating the success you have experienced in your career into more Freedom of time and the ability to live life on your terms, and the ability to weather economic volatility and uncertainty.

It is the pathway off the hamster wheel.

As Warren Buffett famously said . . .

"If you don't find a way to make money while you sleep, you will work until you die."

CHAPTER TWO

Building Your Economic Hurricane Survival Plan

Our current financial and economic state can seem overwhelming and depressing. In my experience, action is the most effective antidote against fear and uncertainty.

Now is the time to take responsibility for your future and the future of those you love. You can take it a step at a time and fight back as an individual or, better yet, as a family. You can empower yourself to protect your wealth and autonomy by making practical moves.

Here is my personal financial preparation checklist for weathering economic storms. In the next chapter I'll expand on investing strategies for a market downturn or economic upheaval. But first, I want to share with you the following checklist to get your own financial house in order.

Economic Storm Preparation Checklist

☐ Manage Your Burn Rate

High income does not equal high net worth. High income individuals are notorious for living paycheck to paycheck. This is especially true for medical practitioners who feel that they have earned the right to a certain lifestyle or who feel pressured by society and their peers to maintain that lifestyle.

Be wary of letting others define what "success" looks like. Keeping up with the Joneses is not a game worth winning. I speak with dozens of doctors who learn this lesson the hard way much too late in life.

> **Be wary of letting others define what "success" looks like. Keeping up with the Joneses is not a game worth winning.**

It is essential to keep a firm grip on your financial "burn rate" (what you spend each month to fund your lifestyle). There should be a significant margin between what you earn and what you spend. The difference should be managed and invested wisely. Focus on productive, income-generating assets, such as real estate, which retain value and appreciate over time.

The key? Differentiate between expenses and investments. Every penny directed toward a future that grows in value is a step closer to genuine ownership and individual sovereignty.

❏ Reduce and Eliminate Debt

In periods of economic growth, long term fixed rate debt can be a powerful tool for growth. However, in periods of economic turmoil, debt becomes a double edged sword. It can limit your options and Freedom, and put your financial security at risk.

Debt should never be used to expand your lifestyle. When possible, it should be strategically reduced and eliminated. Priority should be placed on reducing exposure to variable rate debt as it places your future financial obligations beyond your control.

❏ Maintain Sufficient "Dry Powder" and Liquidity

In the event of an economic crisis, financial liquidity gives you the ability to adapt and reposition. It gives you optionality.

In times of economic growth, it is prudent to maximize every opportunity to make your dollars work hard for you. In times of economic contraction, the preservation of capital is the priority. Success can be measured in losses *not* suffered. Cash or cash equivalents are one form of strategic investment.

Today, there are numerous opportunities to park capital on a short term basis for higher returns than we've seen in recent history. As this book is written, short term U.S. Treasury Bills are paying over 5%. Many banks are offering high yield savings accounts, and money market accounts offer comparable returns. Cash can be stored on a short term basis with minimal risk exposure. I discuss these options in more detail in a subsequent chapter.

> **Today, there are numerous opportunities to park capital on a short term basis for higher returns than we've seen in recent history.**

I also discuss investment asset classes that are best suited to periods of economic contraction and volatility. There are opportunities in any stage of the market cycle.

However, consideration should be given to maintaining sufficient cash or cash equivalents in periods of economic upheaval and correction.

This reduces risk exposure to the losses that will be incurred in the downturn of the market cycle. It also creates more optionality for providing for yourself and your family, as well as positioning oneself to take advantage of opportunities that will materialize on the other side of a correction.

Some might argue that cash holdings are exposed to the risk of inflation. This is true. However, this can be mitigated through using "liquid" cash equivalents as a place of higher ground until new opportunities arrive to move investments back into tangible equities such as businesses and/or real estate holdings.

Personally, I am at a stage of life and career where capital preservation is of greater priority vs compounding growth. I would rather live to fight another day. Each investor must choose allocations for their own portfolio.

Invest in Real, Tangible Assets

It's not just about having money in the bank. Wealthy individuals worldwide have always understood the importance of accumulating tangible assets like real estate and land, indicating its timeless value. Tangible assets can hedge against inflation and maintain value through periods of economic upheaval. But to truly step into ownership, you must transition from mere expenses (such as your primary residence) to genuine investments.

We will discuss more of this in the coming chapters.

❏ Increase Business Resiliency

It is essential for business owners to create margin and prepare to adapt.

Now is a time to be wary of major growth, expansion, or taking on large amounts of additional debt. Focus should be put on maintaining profit margins and sufficient cash reserves to weather 6–12 months of financial disruption.

Make sure you have the ability to pay down any open lines of credit. Pay them off quickly as variable rates will make them go up. Or go back to the lender and turn those into amortizing fixed rate loans that you can pay off over a number of years. When credit tightens in a recession market, any lines of credit (credit cards, HELOCs, etc.) can be called. You are at the mercy of the lender. Don't think it can't happen to you. Those kinds of loans legally allow the lender to call your loan with little notice. If you are utilizing open lines of credit, you are vulnerable to this threat.

Look for resilient revenue streams. A recession means people will cut back on goods, services, and products that they don't deem essential. How can you still keep people in your "funnel?" Dental offices (the smart ones) are offering patients who are not on insurance a prepaid membership with certain services bundled in as a way to give them a discount and retain their clientele. The winners will continue to innovate on ideas such as this.

Learn to communicate. Create a message that resonates deeply with your customers and network. Look for strategic collaborations with people who align with your message and mission. Build strong, resilient relationships with customers/patients as well as team, key suppliers and others. Relationships are your most valuable business asset.

> *Relationships are your most valuable business asset.*

⌴ Preserve Business Equity

Next up is business equity. Whether you're an entrepreneur or an employee, the concept remains consistent: Own a piece of the pie. For business owners, it's all about understanding your assets. Know and protect your business's value, especially during challenging times. Ensure you have an exit strategy and assets that can serve as a safety net or alternative currency.

Beware of banking any exit strategy on promised future recaps or payments that are dependent on economic performance in the future. Often those assumptions are based on linear extrapolation—assumptions of future growth based on the recent past. This does not account for the impact of changing economic conditions in the future.

⌑ Create a Personal Family Emergency Plan

Make your preparation plan. Take the time to plan in case the worst outcomes come to pass. You don't expect a fire, but if there is one, you have an escape plan and insurance policy in place before it happens.

In the event of economic / social collapse: Is there a location that you would go to with others who are prepared and willing to cooperate? Communication may be limited. What alternatives are in place?

Engage with an estate planning attorney to discuss utilizing trusts for your assets or gifting them to loved ones while you are still alive. If a Central Bank Digital Currency is implemented, how would you continue business if your access to funds was suspended for some time? Do you have small denominations of precious metals or something else? Ammo. Crypto. Cash at home. What about your "Black Book" with critical contacts, instructions, and passwords? Think through these things today so that you can more easily address any periods of financial or geopolitical chaos in the future.

⌑ Create Relational Resiliency

Relationships are your greatest insurance policy. Special attention should be given to strong connections with your inner circle—what I call "Your five." A network or tribe with whom you share values and trust. Collective resources are much greater than the limits of the soloist. Finding or intentionally creating a network of people you know, like, and most importantly, can trust will be essential. Don't wait to begin or enhance your current relationships.

> **Collective resources are much greater than the limits of the soloist. Finding or intentionally creating a network of people you know, like, and most importantly, can trust will be essential.**

Lessons in Wealth Preservation and Freedom from the World's Wealthiest Families

Do what they do, not what they say. The elite are buying up real estate and other tangible assets. Central banks and wealthy individuals are adding to their gold and precious metals reserves, making sure to own assets that retain or increase in value. Follow their actions.

> **The elite are buying up real estate and other tangible assets. Central banks and wealthy individuals are adding to their gold and precious metals reserves, making sure to own assets that retain or increase in value. Follow their actions.**

Diversify your assets and financial portfolio. Shifts in the global financial order could have a range of possible catalysts and outcomes, and we don't know the timeline. You must have a diversified, hedged, and resilient portfolio to prepare for worst-case scenarios.

As traditional ideas of ownership evolve (i.e. the World Economic Forum's 2030 prediction, "You will own nothing and be happy"), tangible assets, diversified investments, and business equity remain paramount. By understanding these changes and proactively taking informed steps, you can navigate this rapidly changing world, protecting your personal rights and maintaining a sense of sovereignty over your destiny.

CHAPTER THREE

How to De-risk Your Portfolio

For most professionals and business owners who have spent a lifetime following the typical Wall Street retirement advice, the question becomes . . .

"How do I take control of my investments and how do I move to higher ground?"

This question takes on even greater significance in the face of a pending recession. In a bull market filled with easy government money (such as what we've experienced for the past 14 years), everyone looks like a genius. You can throw a dart at just about any "investment" and make money, because a rising tide lifts all boats.

But as Warren Buffet famously said . . . *"Only when the tide goes out do you discover who's been swimming naked."*

The tide will not rise forever. When it recedes, change happens fast. In the contraction phase of the market cycle, capital preservation is key. To minimize the risk of losing your capital in a market correction, you must look for investments that have greater underlying protection and lower downside risk.

> **When it recedes, change happens fast. In the contraction phase of the market cycle, capital preservation is key.**

Moving to Higher Ground

⌴ Precious Metals

Historically, gold has been an excellent currency hedge when the dollar weakens. While precious metals may appreciate in value over time, they do not create cash flow. They serve primarily as a value preservation vs income producing investment. However, with more advanced strategies such as ratio trading, it is possible to create significant growth over long periods of time.

There are numerous ways to acquire and maintain ownership or possession of precious metals. While delegating the storage and security of precious metals holdings can come with significant convenience, consideration should also be given to the control and optionality gained by taking physical possession of a smaller amount of precious metals. In the event of a societal breakdown, you can't barter with precious metals you do not have possession of.

☐ Treasuries and Income Producing Cash Equivalents

In the current high-rate and high-interest economy, money markets, CDs, and treasuries are comparatively low risk and provide a much higher return then they ever have in recent history (4–5.5%). I personally have invested significantly in treasuries, which are backed by the US government—about as safe as you can be right now.

However, over the long run these accounts don't generate the returns you need to offset inflation and future higher costs of living. Inflation, which continues to impact American lives at a massive scale, runs at a much higher rate than the official government's CPI stats. The metrics have changed many times over the years to try to reduce the perception of inflation.

Taxes, already high, will continue to rise. If you factor in the taxes you will need to pay in the future and the decrease in your financial buying power from inflation, you would need double-digit returns to sustain your wealth and accommodate the cost of living in the future.

Where are you going to get that on a predictable and reliable basis? Is the stock market going to continue to produce that? No. A common fallacy is to believe that past performance indicates future results. Most financial advisors haven't lived through an economic cycle like we are going through—the closest correlation is the stagflation of the 70s and 80s.

> **Most financial advisors haven't lived through an economic cycle like we are going through— the closest correlation is the stagflation of the 70s and 80s.**

In times of stagflation, market returns will be much more nominal, at best. At worst, we face a major market reset of historic proportions. Can you afford to weather another "lost decade" for stocks? How about a market contraction of 40–50% such as we saw in the 2008 financial crisis?

But if not the stock market . . . where can investors turn to hedge against inflation?

Securing Wealth with Real, Tangible Assets

The wealthiest people in the world are landowners—investing in "the earth." Land is one of the best preservers of wealth. Raw land (land that is not income-producing) is an ideal investment for those who don't need or require additional cash flow. Land will hold value and offset the inflationary forces that will be significant in the years and decades ahead.

Bill Gates is buying farmland. His portfolio has expanded to over 268,000 acres in the past few years. He is not the only billionaire buying up land. Others have surpassed him.

- Jeff Bezos has amassed 400,000 acres
- Ted Turner (media billionaire) owns a staggering 2,000,000 acres

Many of the billionaires buying up US land are *not* US citizens. Foreign entities own over 43.4 million acres of US farm and timberland. That number has grown dramatically just in the past few years.

> **Many of the billionaires buying up US land are not US citizens. Foreign entities own over 43.4 million acres of US farm and timberland. That number has grown dramatically just in the past few years.**

Let that sink in for a moment.

Personal wealth and the freedom and autonomy accompanying it come from what you "own." That is how generational wealth is sustained through periods of upheaval. It is also how wealth is passed from generation to generation. Property. Real assets. No enduring family dynasty was ever built on a 401k. Wealth is created from the ownership of assets that increase in value over time.

The wealthy are buying up the ground beneath our feet.

Other "earthly" investments would include commodities, precious metals, fossil fuels, timber, improved real estate that sits directly on land, and businesses—with either active or passive involvement.

This is why I love tangible assets. Through tangible assets like real estate (as well as businesses which you own and control), there are opportunities to create sustainable cash flow, as well as the chance to ride through economic storms and take advantage of opportunities in their wake. In addition, tangible assets provide a measure of control. With tangible assets, you can both create cash flow as well as create an equity hedge against the ravages of inflation.

> **With tangible assets, you can both create cash flow as well as create an equity hedge against the ravages of inflation.**

I love real estate, but not all real estate is the same. When most people think of real estate investing, they think of buying local rental properties in their neighborhood. I call this becoming an "accidental landlord." Is it a viable model for some? Yes. But make no mistake, it is not "passive." Nor is it suited to every stage of the market cycle. Right now, it is very difficult to find properly priced residential real estate in most markets.

Different asset classes are better suited to various market conditions. There are numerous ways to become a passive investor in real estate assets without the headache and time commitment of ownership—for example, hard money lending, or partnering with other investors on a larger scale in funds or syndications.

Because real estate is so localized and inefficient, the small investors (you and me) are able to access certain opportunities that the major REITs on Wall Street simply cannot take advantage of.

The advantage of cash flow producing tangible assets lies in their ability to ride through economic volatility. I was personally heavily invested in single family homes in the great financial crisis of 2008. While the value of the assets I owned fluctuated during that time period, the rents remained steady. I continued to generate positive cash flow on a sustainable and predictable basis. On the other side of the crisis, I was positioned to take advantage of the numerous opportunities to buy assets at a deep discount.

I personally doubled my net worth in the few short years that followed the 2008 downturn (more about this in Chapter 5).

DIY vs Strategic Collaboration—the Pathway to Passive Investing

The key to accessing these opportunities is relationships. I've often said, "Your network is your net worth." You can learn real estate from the ground up, figuring it out as you go and learning by trial and error. This takes many years, but you could do it—that's the way I started in the 1980s.

Today, I don't want to do all that work, but I still want to mitigate the risk of where I put my money.

Rather than doing everything on my own like I did when I first started, I now invest my money through other people with whom I've built trust and relationships. I've vetted these individuals and understand where the opportunities lie. We collaborate to form a mutually beneficial partnership for each opportunity (this is what investing is).

> **Rather than doing everything on my own like I did when I first started, I now invest my money through other people with whom I've built trust and relationships.**

Collaborating with other trusted experts can make a big difference, but you need to find the right place with the right group to learn how to do this.

Becoming your own financial advocate means not delegating decisions to anyone else (advisors, CPAs, fund managers, etc.) It means working with others to make the best decisions for your money. This is how you de-risk your portfolio.

You can't follow the herd. Safety will never be found in the common markets. The key is to understand the market cycles and how you can hedge for each market iteration. This is different from trying to time the market. I'm advocating for hedging your risk. It is possible to adapt to the broad movements of the markets and "ride the waves" without trying to time exactly what will happen next. Do you know how to do that? Would you like to learn?

Your dedication and hard work brought you to your current pinnacle of success. You can do the same with your money, but you have to take the steps to learn how to do it. You don't need to go back to school to get an MBA in finance, real estate, or anything else. But you do need to invest the time and effort into becoming a well educated investor.

As I have aged, I value "speed to goal" more and more. Rather than spending years / decades learning a new skill by myself, I would rather partner with someone who has already "been there and done that" so I can get to my end goal much faster.

CHAPTER FOUR

How to Conduct Due Diligence Amidst Market Upheaval

There's a story that in 1929, Joseph Kennedy, the father of the late U.S. President, John F. Kennedy, conversed with a shoeshine boy on a street in New York City where he lived.

The shoeshine boy expressed excitement as he offered Mr. Kennedy some unsolicited stock tips.

At that moment, Joe knew he needed to sell. When the shoeshine boys offer stock tips, it's time to get out of the market. He sold off his entire stock portfolio. The crash came soon after, leaving him with his wealth intact at a time when many others lost theirs in the Great Depression.

True or not, this scenario—whether shoeshine boys, Uber drivers, or even doctors—plays out regularly toward the end of every rising economic and market cycle. It's no different this time.

This is the "Euphoria" phase of the market cycle.

Over the past five to seven years, I have observed a proliferation of new sponsors and promoters selling real estate to private investors. These promotions often come in the form of large syndications (multi-family or commercial projects) or real estate funds that function as private Real Estate Investment Trusts (REITs). They are touted by promoters (sometimes even doctors) who have very little or no previous experience or track record in the world of real estate and no experience going through a full market cycle.

They have changed the landscape of real estate investing and must be addressed in any discussion of moving investments toward real, tangible assets. The risks and complexities are compounding in this new reality.

I understand the incentives and motivation. In every cycle, as the bull run (upswing) nears the top, anyone and everyone who has watched from the sidelines, or participated passively, decides that they want a bigger piece of the action. And why not? The greed factor, which is part of what makes capitalism and opportunities flourish in a free market, attracts people and entrepreneurs who want "in" on the fun.

> *In every cycle, as the bull run (upswing) nears the top, anyone and everyone who has watched from the sidelines, or participated passively, decides that they want a bigger piece of the action. And why not?*

There is nothing illegal here; it is simply a sign of the times. As long as the upward market cycle continues unabated, many of these syndications and funds work out okay—some even do relatively well. As the saying goes, "Everyone is a genius in a bull market."

The problem is that, eventually, the music stops and so do the investment operators. It's happening as we speak. And we've only begun the market correction/recession that has been anticipated by those who keep a close eye on the fundamentals of the economy, interest rates, the bond market, the banking sector, and credit liquidity. Everything is in massive flux, creating the warnings herein.

When projects go south, as many will in the near future, the promoters and the sponsor-operators have already made their upfront fees. Many of the bank loans are nonrecourse, meaning there is no liability for the sponsor and promoters to walk away from the deal and claim, "We made our best efforts."

Because the legal representations are so well-written to protect the sponsors and promoters, there is no recourse to the limited partner investors unless malfeasance or misappropriation of funds has occurred. The latter requires a legal fight, which can be expensive and protracted.

The bottom line is that, as a passive limited partner, you have very little in the way of remedies once you have invested and signed off on the legal offering documents. The promoters have minimal risk, if any.

Due Diligence—Vetting the "Who" and the "How" of Prospective Investments

If you are going to be a passive investor in real estate (vs being an active house flipper or landlord), success is all about working with the right people. It's about knowing how to build successful collaborations and knowing how to properly structure those collaborations in a way that creates proper incentive and transparency for all parties.

Most syndications are structured to be managed by one or more "General Partners" (GPs). They are the operators responsible for the orchestration and management of the deal. Investors who play the role of Limited Partners usually provide the capital.

In 2012, Congress passed significant legislation allowing GPs to market and promote private investment opportunities without being registered and licensed by the Securities and Exchange Commission.

Since then, real estate syndications have become ubiquitous. There is very little oversight of the marketing claims, promises, or past history of those who are offering investment opportunities.

Today, there are even many doctors and professional practitioners who are signing on to become "Co-GP Promoters"—partnering with a fund or syndication to help raise capital (in exchange for hefty commissions). Often, these "Co-GP Promoters" have little previous experience or track record in real estate. They become General Partners to lend credibility in the eyes of colleagues and give the deal sponsors access to groups of high-net-worth investors (doctors, other practice professionals) to whom they would not otherwise have access.

> **Today, there are even many doctors and professional practitioners who are signing on to become "Co-GP Promoters"—partnering with a fund or syndication to help raise capital (in exchange for hefty commissions).**

Who are the General Partners, the actual operators? They could be anyone, and here is where the danger appears. Exactly what is the vetting or due diligence being done by the Co-GP promoter? Other than a relationship connection with all of the incentives geared towards the promoters . . . no real underwriting occurs. It takes time and expense, and during market hype, no one ever asks.

Sure, there will be talk of prior track records, but at the end of a market cycle, prior track records are of little relevance. Many sponsor operators have never experienced a full market cycle in their performance. That would be the first good question to ask, but nobody does. The assumption is that the promises of IRRs (Internal Rate of Return—which is how all such equity syndications are sold), in the high teens to high twenty percents, are as good as guaranteed.

Alas, these are only projections often based on very faulty assumptions. Again, not illegal. However, understand that the sponsor-operators hire the very best attorneys to write their PPMs (private placement memorandums) and Operating Agreements, which essentially dispel them from any liability for lack of performance outside of verified fraud.

As an "accredited investor," the SEC (Securities and Exchange Commission), assumes that you are wise enough and have the resources to do proper due diligence. But do you? Do you have that experience? Do you have the capital resources to perform adequate financial and legal underwriting, including full background checks on each principal sponsor?

> **As an "accredited investor," the SEC (Securities and Exchange Commission), assumes that you are wise enough and have the resources to do proper due diligence. But do you?**

The answer is "no." Not only do you not have those resources, but you're too busy to take the time, and that is what all promoters are counting on . . . plus the greed factor. Fear of Missing Out (FOMO)—you don't want to miss this opportunity because you've felt you've missed out too many times in the past.

The fees assessed for these capital-raising efforts are substantial. It is common that the GPs have little or none of their own capital in the deal. This creates a model where GPs are incentivized based on the amount of capital raised (more capital = more fees), rather than the success and sustainability of the investment itself. They don't have any personal stakes in seeing the deal through.

Early in the creation of Freedom Founders, I was advised by some to pursue this route. It is a very lucrative model. There are numerous doctors (on social media and elsewhere) making a fortune by selling these investments, which they often know very little about. I do not need to name names. Many of you know who they are and can easily find them.

By contrast, I do not sell real estate or any securities, and I do not have any financial interest in the investments my members choose. The reason I have and will continue to stay away from the "Co-GP Promoter" model has to do with mal-incentives.

The Importance of Aligning Incentives

The fundamental issue with the Co-GP Promoter model lies in its inherent mal-incentives:

- **Fee-Driven Compensation**: Co-GP Promoters typically earn fees based on the capital they raise and transaction fees for putting the deal together. There is an incentive to focus on quantity over quality. They always need a new deal to promote.

- **Lack of Skin in the Game**: Without a significant personal stake in the investment outcomes, Co-GP Promoters may not be as invested in the project's long-term success.

- **Misalignment with Investor Interests**: The primary focus on capital raising can lead to a misalignment between what's best for the investor and what benefits the Co-GP Promoter.

- **Propensity to "Oversell" Returns**: Because the sponsors often make the majority of their fees upfront, they are incentivized to gloss over risks and oversell potential returns. Their compensation is not dependent on making good on those promises.

This structure is nothing new. It has been used for decades in network marketing. It has simply been retooled to sell investment products to high-net-worth investors.

Network marketing = selling products to friends/colleagues for a commission, often products that you do not or would not use yourself.

The proliferation of Co-GP Promoters in the investment sphere has several implications for investors.

- **Increased Risk Exposure**: Investors may find themselves exposed to higher risks as Co-GP Promoters might not thoroughly vet opportunities with the investors' best interests in mind.

- **Diluted Returns**: It's common for these deals to be fee-driven on the front end. If the sponsors are receiving their profit on the front end, this reduces overall returns for investors.

- **Lack of Control and Leverage**: If the sponsors are making their profit on the front end of the deal, they have little incentive to manage well or stick with the project if complications arise. This means that if things don't go according to plan, investors have very little leverage to ensure accountability and follow-through from the deal's sponsors.

Resisting the Siren Call of Big Returns

Often real estate promoters are selling deals touting larger-than-life returns. Big promises, especially for where we are in the current market cycle.

Larger-than-life returns are tempting. Isn't bigger always better?

Without a clear plan and defined strategy for your investing, you WILL be vulnerable to the seductive promises of big wins to create more perceived certainty in your financial future. Without a defined plan, "more" will always seem like a pathway to certainty. But beware. Chasing yield is a fool's errand. It is not a path to certainty but rather to risk. You cannot bank your future on beating the markets for the long haul. Successful investors are often those who are the most disciplined to resist the temptation to chase yield, and instead, pursue a focused strategy of consistent, sustainable returns combined with risk mitigation. This does not happen by accident—a defined plan is needed.

> **Without a defined plan, "more" will always seem like a pathway to certainty. But beware. Chasing yield is a fool's errand.**

Your Financial Blueprint should provide clarity in the following areas:

- **Setting Clear Goals**: Establishing what you want to achieve with your investments, both in the short term and the long term.

- **Risk Management**: Understanding the root causes of risk, assessing the level of risk you're comfortable with, and choosing investment opportunities that align with your goals.

- **Diversification**: Spreading your investments across various assets to mitigate risk and ensure a more stable return over time.

- **Continuous Education**: Keeping abreast of market trends, investment strategies, and financial planning to make informed decisions.

My "Under the Hood" Checklist for Any Investment

Investors looking to discern quality from salesmanship should focus their due diligence in the following areas:

- **Seek Alignment of Interests**: Look for investment opportunities where the incentives of all parties involved are aligned with the success and sustainability of the project.

- **Demand Transparency**: Insist on clear, transparent communication regarding fees, the structure of the investment, and the long-term strategy.

- **Compare Fee Structures**: Don't just assume or take it on faith that fees are "industry normative." Research and get counsel. Consider whether the fee structure properly incentivizes the sponsor to ensure the project is profitable for investors.

- **Beware of Affiliated Party Relationships**: Read or have someone competent review the legal offering and look for affiliate commissions and payouts that may strip the distributions to you, the passive limited partner.

- **Understand Your Rights as a Limited Partner**: Understand the scope of control that the GP and Co-GP have and under what circumstances they can be overruled or replaced if needed.

- **Educate Yourself**: Arm yourself with knowledge about different investment models and their implications to make the most informed decisions.

- **Look for Long-Term Players**: Evaluate the experience of all GPs in the deal and look for operators doing business for the long-haul; building collaborative relationships with long-term, full-cycle operators is the pathway to success and profitability.

Becoming Your Own Financial Advocate

I do believe that hardworking, high-income professionals and business owners need a Plan B investment blueprint outside of their primary source of income—and at least a portion of their investment portfolio allocated in alternative, tangible assets (as opposed to Wall Street financial products). You achieved your success by relying on yourself throughout your many years of education, training, and perseverance to build your career. Why would you not do the same for the money that you earn and then invest?

> **You achieved your success by relying on yourself throughout your many years of education, training, and perseverance to build your career. Why would you not do the same for the money that you earn and then invest?**

Advocating for your own financial destiny rather than relying on third parties to "invest for you" does require a level of dedication and study. I call it a "reinvestment period"—a reinvestment of time and money to learn skill sets that will provide you with the security and peace of mind that you won't run out of money during your retirement years. (Or the reality that your lifestyle has to be reduced.)

Despite the urging of some, I chose a different approach from the beginning. I do not sell real estate. I do not take commissions. My mission and goal is to help colleagues develop the knowledge and skills to become their own financial advocates, as I did. I invest right alongside my members. As a community, we attract, curate, and vet quality operators who have a proven track record and are willing to put their money where their mouth is.

I love helping colleagues become sophisticated investors who have the abilities and the relationships needed to create sustainable cash flow for years and decades to come.

No one else will care about your hard-earned capital as much as you will. The path to Freedom for anyone who wants to ditch the traditional Wall Street model in favor of alternative investments is to make the re-investments needed to educate yourself and find a tribe you can trust.

The path to Freedom is never walked alone!

CHAPTER FIVE

How to Position for Opportunities from Chaos

I started my Plan B investing program in 1980 while a D1 in dental school.

This was not a plan to "get rich quick" or see how fast I could exit the dental chair as a practice owner. At the time I just knew that real estate made sense to me. It was an investment class I could understand and control.

But it wasn't until decades later that the stars aligned for me . . .

In 2008, 28 years after I started investing, all of my hard work, relationship building and market knowledge paid off. 2008 was the start of the Global Financial Crisis. Contraction. Deflation. Everything (all assets) went on sale in America.

And there I was. Ready.

In the next six years I more than doubled my net worth through real estate acquisition. I was able to buy when others were selling. No competition. I had access to private capital and I knew how to put deals together.

> *In the next six years I more than doubled my net worth through real estate acquisition. I was able to buy when others were selling.*

As I write this today, it's time again. Perhaps a generational opportunity is right in front of us.

We are currently in the starting phase of a market correction. If it were not for the manipulations of the politically powerful, I believe it would already be well underway. But we know how the government, the Federal Reserve, and the Treasury collude to manipulate the monetary system.

The government will keep kicking negative effects down the road until they can't anymore. They've been doing so by floating the economy on debt. All the spending and credit expansion that we have experienced has prolonged the inevitable. There will be a correction. It is long overdue.

Why am I telling you this? Because the same behavior and response occur every time there's a major correction. In 2008, no one saw it coming. Even the Federal Reserve Chairman at the time, Bernanke, said, "Housing is all fine. It's all good."

Does this sound familiar?

What we read in the journals, business news, and mainstream media is orchestrated to try to calm the waters. My job is to prepare you for the storm they say isn't coming.

Are You Ready for the Coming Opportunities?

The good news is that after every storm, there are always opportunities for those who are prepared for them. Here are a few questions to help you prepare:

- Where's your capital base today?

- Have you moved your money out of the market and onto higher ground? (See Chapter 3 on de-risking your portfolio).

- Have you self-directed any retirement accounts in order to invest in alternatives like real estate?

- Do you have "dry powder" (liquid capital) set aside to be able to take advantage of opportunities that these changes will create?

Having capital will be critical for funding opportunities. The banks won't be lending. In times of economic crisis, credit contracts. Lines of credit are called. This limits the pool of buyers because most asset acquisitions are structured with leverage. Possessing liquidity will allow you to move quickly and take advantage of once in a lifetime opportunities. This is what I call a Life Inflection point—the opportunity for a major uptick in one's wealth trajectory. Once the correction hits and assets start going on sale, it will be too late to make the appropriate moves. This is your opportunity to get ready and make the most of what's coming.

> **Possessing liquidity will allow you to move quickly and take advantage of once in a lifetime opportunities. This is what I call a Life Inflection point—the opportunity for a major uptick in one's wealth trajectory.**

You need access points. You need a network. Real estate is all about who you know. In addition, you need enough education to understand how to conduct your own due diligence on opportunities (and ideally access to a group that helps facilitate high-level vetting).

It's not a time to be dismal or get depressed. It's a time to prepare, get educated, and build your network. We can't control what the markets do. We can't control what the government does. What we can control is how prepared we are to weather the economic storm and buy assets on the other side.

I more than doubled my net worth after the 2008 Financial Crisis. You can do the same, but you have to be prepared.

CHAPTER SIX

This Time IS Different... Secular Cycles and the Coming Economic Tsunami

In the last 40 years, we have experienced a long-term secular wave of decreasing interest rates. It started back in the 1980s during the Reagan era. It was the beginning of a tremendous amount of growth in all financial products: Wall Street, technology, and even in real estate.

All asset classes benefited greatly from the low cost of capital fueled by decreasing interest rates. It was hard to make an investment and *not* make money.

Fast forward to after the 2008 Great Financial Recession, and the Federal Reserve and Congress injected a huge amount of stimulus into the economy.

Quadruple that for when COVID struck in 2020. Trillions of dollars were injected into the economy. This printed money, fiat currency, had to go somewhere so it went into financial products—like Wall Street and real estate.

> **Trillions of dollars were injected into the economy. This printed money, fiat currency, had to go somewhere so it went into financial products—like Wall Street and real estate.**

It also went into private equity, which was consolidating businesses left and right—even in the field of dentistry. We've seen it in other industries too, but dentistry is what I am familiar with and can dive deeper into.

Many pundits say we're not going to have a recession. *"Everything is back to normal. Interest rates will come down. The Federal Reserve will come to the rescue again and will decrease interest rates. We just have to go through this little gap here. Don't worry about it. It's all okay."*

Beware of wishful thinking. The Fed can only kick the can so far down the road before they run out of road.

These long-wave secular trends in interest rates don't change overnight. There will be volatility with interest rates staying higher for a longer period of time. The last trend I mentioned above lasted 40 years. How long do you think this one will last?

The Rise in Interest Rates Will Affect All Equities and Commodities

The long-term effect of higher interest rates could cause the entire financial arena, especially equities on

Wall Street like stocks, bonds, mutual funds, and ETFs, to undergo a correction.

Even though technology has been riding high, it too is due for a reversion to the mean. Real estate, primarily commercial real estate but even residential, will undergo a correction. This has been a long time coming.

The rising cost of capital, driven by higher interest rates, suggests that the status quo will not continue to exist in the business sector, including in health care.

This includes veterinary medicine, dentistry, and other healthcare industries where private equity buyouts have been occurring with the highest multiples in history. It's been a heyday. Young docs have been taking chips off the table and becoming millionaires, essentially overnight. But the structures of these deals, even from those sold in the last year, are not going to play out the way private equity has promised.

> **Young docs have been taking chips off the table and becoming millionaires, essentially overnight. But the structures of these deals, even from those sold in the last year, are not going to play out the way private equity has promised.**

Why?

It all depends on the cost of capital. Real estate syndications, especially the ones commonly promoted with high IRR return on capital of 16–22%, have relied heavily on the lower cost of capital. Many of their models were predicated on the assumption that future buyers could finance the acquisition at cheap interest rates. But now that things have changed, they won't be able to follow through on their promises.

The run rate for the last three years was, "Jump in. We've got another great deal coming." You would be wise to resist that FOMO because unless you know the operator runs a tight ship, and knows how to minimize risk in a deal, you'll shortly be running on air.

That's what these operators are doing. They're running on air, and most of these deals will fall apart. Even people who have great intentions and have a good track record won't know how to deal with these changes unless they have full cycle experience. Most operators have never seen the backside of an upcycle and don't know what to change in their deal structures to be successful and profitable during a downcycle.

The same thing will happen in the dental industry with the big multiple DSO buyouts. Too many naive docs have jumped at the chance to take a bite of the poisoned apple. They don't know there will not be a second bite. If their promised capital ever does come, it's going to be decreased and delayed way down the road.

Why? Because of the cost of capital. The ability to get these rollups and these recaps is based on the low cost of capital we had over the last 15 years.

That has now changed, and will not be going back down any time soon.

The Risk of Recency Bias in Determining Future Strategy

In the last decade, if you've owned or invested in any tangible assets or financial products with the potential for equity growth, you've likely seen significant gains. This was a period of substantial expansion, where profits came more easily due to favorable market conditions.

The danger, however, lies in assuming that this upward trend is the norm. Recency bias—the tendency to believe that recent patterns will persist—can lead to false confidence in the future. It's a fallacy to think that past performance indicates future results. Relying on a single time period or pattern, with the assumption that it can predict the future, is misguided. Linear extrapolation fails to account for the inherent unpredictability of the world we live in today.

> **Recency bias—the tendency to believe that recent patterns will persist—can lead to false confidence in the future. It's a fallacy to think that past performance indicates future results.**

The reality is that the returns of the last decade are the result of significant manipulation of the markets and economy. The Fed has injected steroids into the economy with little regard for the consequences.

The current national debt has nearly doubled in the last 15 years and the rate of growth is accelerating. It currently sits at $35.09 trillion but we are adding another $1 trillion every 90–100 days.

We are entering dangerous new territory.

"They say they are a pair of bureaucrats who are just as important to the planet as any other life form."

Yet, I see many who treat the last decade of growth as a promise of continued prosperity. They've thrived in the real estate market and confidently proclaim:

"Don't worry about higher interest rates. Don't be concerned with a sluggish economy. Just invest—whether in funds, syndications, or single-family rentals. Real estate and the stock market always appreciate in the long term."

But this assumption—that past performance ensures future growth—is dangerous. Just because real estate values have risen over the past few decades does not mean they will continue to do so indefinitely.

The Uncertainty of "How Much Is Enough" in a Fast-Changing World

Retirees have the uncertainty of outliving their retirement savings and no "safe place" for holding their capital. Until recently, there has been no alternative for those who should be more conservative as that investment category has not provided the dividend return necessary to maintain a certain lifestyle standard.

Historically, the wall street model has not had a strong answer to the question of "How much is enough?" How can one plan with certainty when your financial future is tied to the volatility of the markets? The default answer becomes "keep working just a little bit longer . . . "

> *Historically, the wall street model has not had a strong answer to the question of "How much is enough?" How can one plan with certainty when your financial future is tied to the volatility of the markets?*

But without a clear destination, you are likely to remain trapped in practice for years or even decades longer than needed, simply due to uncertainty and the perceived safety of the status quo (trading time for dollars) vs. the unknown of market volatility, inflation eating away at your nest egg, and lack of clarity about the future.

What This Means for You

- More volatility—long runs of economic stability appear to be in the rearview mirror.

- Continued CPI inflation (consumer cost of living) with Asset Deflation (equities, stocks, real estate and business valuation multiples).

- Lower growth—an anemic economy. Quick-turn profits on assets will be few and far between.

Fundamental or metric-based businesses and investments held for longer periods of time will be back in vogue.

In short, you cannot and should not rely on the past performance of any model. It is your responsibility to advocate for your financial future. Failing to do that may lead to an outcome that you are not prepared for or want.

Now is the time to become your own financial advocate. Your future and the future of the next generations depends upon it.

CHAPTER SEVEN

Building a Legacy—an Ark to Preserve Freedom for the Next Generation

When Noah built the ark, he was not merely saving himself. He was preserving his family and life for future generations on the earth. That was the deeper purpose behind his mission and sacrifice.

So many entrepreneurs, business owners and professionals work hard to create a better life for their children. Unfortunately, despite our best efforts and intentions, it is difficult to preserve wealth and build a legacy that lasts.

> *So many entrepreneurs, business owners and professionals work hard to create a better life for their children. Unfortunately, despite our best efforts and intentions, it is difficult to preserve wealth and build a legacy that lasts.*

In the United States, approximately 80% of businesses are closely held, often by families who pour their heart, soul, and sweat into building something valuable. However, most of these businesses fail or are sold before the second generation can take the reins. Only a mere 10% manage to function as privately held enterprises within the same family by the third generation.

This phenomenon is so common that it's encapsulated in the adage: "Shirtsleeves to shirtsleeves in three generations." But why is this the case? And more importantly, how can families break this cycle and ensure their wealth, both financial and otherwise, is preserved across generations?

CREATE

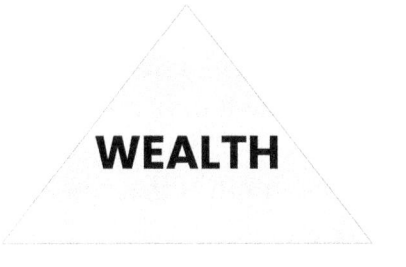

WEALTH

PROTECT   PRESERVE

Wealth Creation: The Foundation of Legacy

At the core of any family's financial legacy is wealth creation. But wealth is far more than just money; it's an intricate tapestry woven from human, intellectual, social, and financial capital.

1. **Human Capital**: This is the family itself—the people, their health, their skills, and their abilities. Investing in education, well-being, and personal development ensures that each family member is equipped to contribute to the family's legacy.

2. **Intellectual Capital**: The knowledge, ideas, and innovations that the family accumulates. This includes the family's business acumen, the lessons learned from past successes

and failures, and the wisdom passed down through generations.

3. **Social Capital**: The relationships and networks that the family builds over time. A robust network of connections can open doors to opportunities that might otherwise remain closed.

4. **Financial Capital**: While often the most visible form of wealth, financial capital is merely a tool. It's what you do with it that matters—how you invest it, how you grow it, and how you use it to support the other forms of capital.

To effectively create and maintain wealth, families must establish non-negotiables—core values that guide every decision. These values should be documented in a family manual that outlines everything from transitions of power to daily rituals. This manual serves as the blueprint for sustaining the family's wealth, both in the business and in investments.

> **To effectively create and maintain wealth, families must establish non-negotiables—core values that guide every decision.**

More important than money is the ability to pass along the values, mindset, work ethic, connections, resources and opportunities to create wealth in the future. That is where the real power lies.

As a wealthy friend of mine with a large family often says . . . "Don't hide the dynamite."

Show them *how* to create wealth—that is where the real power lies. It is the most meaningful legacy of all.

Real Wealth: Beyond the Balance Sheet

True wealth encompasses so much more than just financial assets. It's about the legacy you leave behind, the impact you have on the world, and the lessons you impart to the next generation.

One of my mentors often quotes an old African proverb: "When an old man dies, a library burns." The knowledge, experiences, and stories that each generation holds are invaluable. Preserving these intangible assets is just as crucial as protecting the financial ones.

> **"When an old man dies, a library burns." —African proverb**

Generational wealth, therefore, is the bridge that connects the past, present, and future. It's not just about passing on money but about passing on wisdom, values, and traditions that will sustain the family through the trials and tribulations of life.

Wealth Protection: Building a Fortress Around Your Legacy

Wealth creation is only the first step. The next, equally important step, is wealth protection. This involves careful planning and foresight to ensure that the wealth created is not eroded by poor management or unforeseen circumstances.

'YOU'VE INHERITED THE FAMILY MISFORTUNE'

1. **Estate Planning**: A well-crafted estate plan ensures that wealth is transferred according to your wishes and in the most tax-efficient manner possible.

2. **Integrated Entities and Trusts**: These legal structures can protect assets from creditors, ensure privacy, and provide for future generations.

3. **Insurance**: Life insurance, property insurance, and liability insurance are essential tools for protecting against the unexpected.

4. **Tax Management**: Proper tax planning can minimize the burden on your estate and preserve more wealth for future generations.

5. **Family Office**: For those with substantial wealth, a family office can manage investments, handle administrative tasks, and coordinate all aspects of wealth management.

The Rockefeller family is often contrasted with the Vanderbilts in discussions of wealth preservation. While the Vanderbilts squandered their fortune within a few generations, the Rockefellers established a robust system of stewardship that has preserved their wealth for over a century.

> *While the Vanderbilts squandered their fortune within a few generations, the Rockefellers established a robust system of stewardship that has preserved their wealth for over a century.*

Another lesser known story is the story of Joe Robbie, the founder of the Miami Dolphins.

The Story of Joe Robbie: A Cautionary Tale

The son of Lebanese immigrants, Robbie worked his way through law school and became a successful attorney. His passion for sports, particularly football, led him to co-found the Miami Dolphins in 1966. With limited resources and immense perseverance, Robbie turned the Dolphins into one of the most successful franchises in NFL history, culminating in the team's perfect season in 1972—a feat that remains unmatched to this day.

Robbie's vision extended beyond just building a winning team; he was instrumental in constructing the Dolphins' home, the Miami Dolphins Stadium (now known as Hard Rock Stadium), a project that required immense personal financial commitment. By the time of his death in 1990, Robbie had amassed what many would consider "generational wealth".

The Unraveling of a Legacy

However, his story took a tragic turn after his death. Robbie's estate was valued at around $100 million, a significant sum at the time—but his wealth was largely illiquid, tied up in the ownership of the Dolphins and the stadium. Unfortunately, Robbie had not established a comprehensive estate plan to preserve his wealth and legacy. The lack of liquidity in his estate meant that when the IRS demanded payment of estate taxes—levied at a high rate—his heirs were faced with a difficult choice: Find a way to raise the money, or sell off key assets.

Without sufficient liquid assets to cover the estate taxes, Robbie's heirs were forced to sell the Miami Dolphins and the stadium to pay the tax bill. This marked the beginning of the end for the Robbie family's control over the team that Joe Robbie had worked so hard to build. The sale of the Dolphins for $106 million to Wayne Huizenga, a prominent South Florida businessman, marked the end of the Robbie family's involvement in the NFL and the dissolution of Joe Robbie's legacy.

Seeing Beyond the Horizon of Your Own Life

Joe Robbie's story underscores the importance of proper estate planning, particularly for those whose wealth is tied up in illiquid assets like businesses, real estate, or valuable collectibles. Estate taxes, often referred to as the "death tax," can be a significant burden on heirs, especially when the majority of the estate's value is not easily convertible to cash.

Robbie's case is a powerful reminder that building wealth is only part of the equation. Preserving that wealth and ensuring its smooth transfer to future generations requires meticulous planning and foresight.

Wealth Preservation: The Stewardship of Legacy

Wealth preservation is not just about protecting assets; it's about stewardship. This means managing wealth in a way that benefits not just the current generation but also future ones. It's the difference between being a consumer of wealth and a steward of it.

> **Wealth preservation is the difference between being a consumer of wealth and a steward of it.**

Generational wealth is not a luxury but a responsibility. It's about teaching your children to fish so that they can feed their families for a lifetime, rather than just handing them a fish. This stewardship involves passing the torch, not just of money but of wisdom and values.

A practical tool for passing on true wealth is the **Wealth Preservation Checklist**, included below.

Wealth Preservation Checklist

1. **Agreements and Governance**:

    - **Vision Statement**: Articulating the long-term goals and purpose of the family and their wealth.

    - **Mission Statement**: Defining the immediate objectives and strategies to achieve the family's vision.

    - **Family Constitution**: A formal document that outlines the governance structure, roles, and responsibilities within the family.

2. **Black Book**: Every family should build out its "Black Book"—a collection of key relationships and connections that are vital to the family's ongoing success.

3. **Traditions and Rituals**: These are the glue that holds the family together. Establishing and maintaining traditions ensures that the family's values are passed down through generations.

4. **Photographs and Memories**: Preserving the stories and memories that define the family's identity is crucial. These intangible assets are often what bind the family together across generations.

5. **Preserving the Stories**: Writing down the stories, lessons, and experiences of each generation creates a rich tapestry that future generations can draw upon for guidance and inspiration. Letters, like those from John D. Rockefeller to his son, serve as a timeless bridge between generations.

A Legacy Built on Stewardship

A legacy of wealth is not built in a day, but through consistent dedication and wise choices. The goal is not just to amass monetary wealth but to build something that will last. By focusing on wealth creation, protection, and preservation, families can break the cycle of "shirtsleeves to shirtsleeves in three generations" and establish a legacy that endures for centuries.

> *A legacy of wealth is not built in a day, but through consistent dedication and wise choices. The goal is not just to amass monetary wealth but to build something that will last.*

Generational wealth is more than a financial asset; it's a living testament to the values, wisdom, and dedication of those who came before. It's a responsibility that each generation must embrace, nurture, and pass on.

CONCLUSION: IT CAN'T HAPPEN HERE—WEALTH INTIMIDATION AND LOSS OF AUTONOMY

"The greatest enemy of freedom is not oppression, but indifference."

This quote from Sinclair Lewis's 1935 novel *It Can't Happen Here* resonates even today. It is a stark reminder of the importance of active engagement and vigilance in preserving democratic values and individual liberties.

While oppression is undoubtedly a formidable force, indifference allows such tyrannical ideologies to fester and flourish unchallenged. Through the collective indifference of apathetic citizens, oppressive regimes can solidify their power and curtail the freedoms they claim to protect. This truth compels us to examine our complacency and highlights the urgency of resolute action in the face of encroaching threats to our freedom.

"Power corrupts, and absolute power corrupts absolutely." —Lord Acton

This proverbial saying denotes that one's moral sense decreases as one's power increases. When individuals or groups are granted power, there is a risk that they will abuse it for their gain or become tyrannical in their actions.

All great empires eventually decline. History has shown that excessive expansionism, internal strife, and the failure to address social and economic inequalities can lead to the decline and collapse of even the most powerful empires. Unfortunately, the aggregation of political power is mired within our human DNA. Only the most ethical can resist. America is on that track. It can and will happen here.

Personal wealth and the freedom and autonomy accompanying it come from what you "own." Property. Real assets. Wealth is created from the ownership of assets that increase in value over time. Asset ownership allows people to grow their wealth exponentially, increasing it by several multiples of the original investment. Working and earning alone cannot build wealth.

> **Personal wealth and the freedom and autonomy accompanying it come from what you "own." Asset ownership allows people to grow their wealth exponentially, increasing it by several multiples of the original investment.**

The World Economic Forum's 2030 predictions, including the warning, *"You will own nothing and be happy,"* have profound implications for personal wealth creation. Imagine a world where you don't own a car, a house, appliances, or clothes. This is the future they envision for us.

The idea that you will own nothing is an intentional barrier to individual wealth creation. Throughout history, people who haven't owned property have found themselves unfree, unhappy, and worse. This is a philosophical concern and a real threat to our financial security and future.

People who study history know that the financial order changes regularly. In 2022, President Biden stated, *"We are at an inflection point in the world economy. It occurs every three or four generations . . . and now is a time when things are shifting. There will be a new world order out there, and we've got to lead it."* The World Economic Forum predicts that the U.S. will eventually lose its superpower status.

Wall Street is now renting the American Dream to its citizens. During the Great Recession, while individuals and financial institutions took on too much risk in the housing market, their outcomes differed. Individuals lost homes to foreclosures, while financial institutions received taxpayer-funded bailouts.

The cheap capital from the Fed's years of subsidized "easy money" policies enabled corporations to do something they had never done before: compete with you for a home. This market did not exist before 2010. Approximately twenty percent of the homes sold in various U.S. markets are bought by a Wall Street corporation or hedge fund.

> **Approximately twenty percent of the homes sold in various U.S. markets are bought by a Wall Street corporation or hedge fund.**

These investors aren't house flippers. They want to rent the American dream back to young people who would otherwise be homebuyers. Forcing a renter nation removes families' most significant wealth-creation mechanisms, transferring that wealth from Main Street to Wall Street. Likewise, the wealthiest accumulate more hard assets. The rich and well-connected continue to own real estate assets and assume the wealth generation created by the rents and upward price appreciation of those houses.

Beware of liberal outcries for rules aimed at one class of people. Just like they aren't trying to hire 80,000 IRS agents to go after those who earn over $400,000 annually, neither is the goal to add wealth, estate, and income taxes to come after the ultra-wealthy. The wealthy have connections and are often financial supporters of congressional lawmakers. They can afford high-priced lawyers and accountants to find loopholes. The middle class, which still holds a substantial portion of wealth, doesn't have the means or access to such advisors or services.

Defending Your Freedom and Preparing for an Uncertain Future

It's crucial to understand that you have the power to fight back against these threats to your wealth and autonomy. You must take action now, or you risk losing everything.

In Freedom Founders, we use a framework that I designed a number of years ago called The Five Freedoms.

In some ways, it replicates Maslow's hierarchy of needs, commonly visualized as a pyramid. I use the same pyramid, but I've changed the frameworks to a great extent to make it more applicable to the journey experienced by practitioners today.

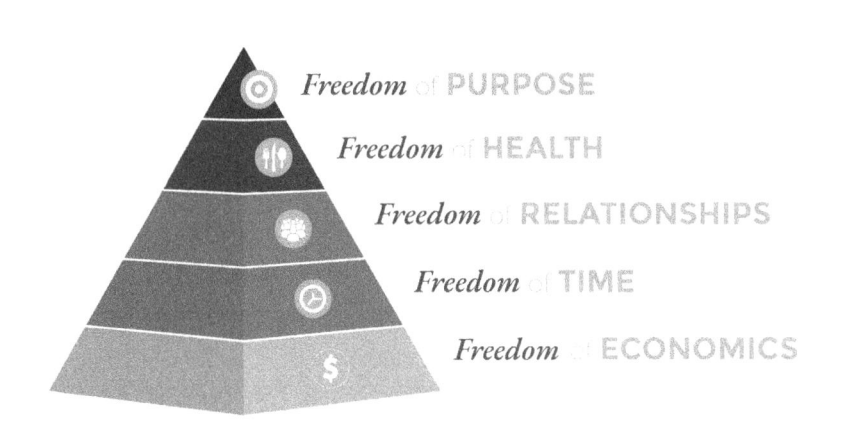

Freedom of PURPOSE
Freedom of HEALTH
Freedom of RELATIONSHIPS
Freedom of TIME
Freedom of ECONOMICS

Here's the pyramid. And as you can see, there are Five Freedoms.

The first Freedom is freedom of finance—economic freedom. The next Freedom is freedom of time. I think that this is, in some cases, the most important one. Next, is freedom of relationships. Fourth is freedom of health. On the top, we have freedom of purpose or significance. This is your real purpose in life, what you're here for, and what gives you meaning. How do you impact the people around you, your community and the world?

Financial Freedom

Financial Freedom is at the base because that's often where we start. That is what many are striving for, especially early in life.

> *Often, we think that financial freedom is a prerequisite for the other freedoms. What many of the doctors I have worked with over the years have discovered is that these freedoms can and should be worked toward simultaneously, not sequentially.*

If you are working toward freedom in these areas of your life, you can evolve to the next phase of your life much sooner than a traditional retirement age (65 or older).

For me personally, I cannot imagine ever retiring in the traditional sense. I'll never stop working in some capacity doing things that are important and meaningful to me. The "work" that I do today is not work. It is what I want to do with my life—a means of creating more impact and significance.

I want you to be in a place to be able to enjoy what you do and do it on your own terms. So many doctors today are in a position where they feel trapped in their work and are stuck in the grind. Sure, they make good money, but is it worth it?

> **I think many doctors would say that they only truly enjoy 15–20% of the work that they do. The rest is clutter and obligations that cause so much brain damage that they would rather live without it.**

I want to flip that ratio for you. I want you to truly enjoy the 80%. Sure, there may always be some minimal aspect of our lives that requires some effort and discipline, but what if that were the significant minority versus the bulk of your time and effort?

What a gift to be able to escape the hamster wheel and truly enjoy the work that you do.

Whether that means changing the dynamics of your practice model, or even a complete exit, seeing a pathway to more freedom can take the pressure off. This does not need to be put off to a distant retirement age or until health issues or burnout force you to the sidelines.

It is important to continue to evolve in your life. We evolved significantly in the early stages of our adult life, re-investing in ourselves through undergrad, dental school, and investment into our practices.

At some point, when did those evolutions and personal transformation slow or come to a halt?

As we evolve through different stages of life, we can progressively elevate upward through the Five Freedoms.

Freedom of Time

> **What is the price of time? Do we sacrifice it today in the hope that time in the future is worth more than today?**

Do we value our current relationships less than those of the future because the future is more important than today?

What is the "price" we pay when we give up or are careless of our time?

We tend to assume that there will be a "future time" when our current sacrifice of time will far outweigh what we are giving up—sacrificing time with our friends, family, community or church.

We give up time making memories—memories that cannot be recreated later for any amount of money.

> **A clear game plan with defined measurables can provide the certainty to start creating more freedom of time now. Today. In many cases, even before total financial freedom has been fully reached.**

For most people, there is never enough certainty to climb beyond the base level of financial freedom. This is why there are high-income professionals still working in their 60s or 70s. The uncertainty creates feelings of guilt and keeps us from giving ourselves permission to live the life we really want to live.

I suffered (as did my family) through the same provocation of "never having enough." I was mistakenly worried that if I didn't constantly work and put in all the hours humanly possible in my business and real estate investments, that I would never get ahead.

The problem is that I had no real plan other than the willingness to work. I worked hard, but not always smart. I was captivated by the journey at the expense of the present, seemingly focused on the future and not on the moment. I know now that one can have both. It requires a different mindset, a different way of thinking and a non-traditional model.

> *What value is money if it cannot buy back control of our time? What value is buying back time if we are no longer young enough to enjoy it?*

Freedom of Relationships

Life is all about relationships. And yet, we put them off. All the money in the world cannot buy back time with those we love. Whether making memories with children in the early years, time with aging parents or extended family, or friendships that bring so much meaning to our lives.

Relationships dissipate over the years. It happens to all of us. But in the end:

> *The relationships and memories made with those we love are our greatest wealth and treasure.*

They are much more meaningful than how much money we made, how big our practice grew, or how big our vacations were.

Quality time is what matters. Freedom of time allows us to invest in building a wealth of relationships.

Freedom of Health

Health is an invaluable asset that empowers us to pursue our aspirations at any stage of life. It serves as a foundation for living fully, allowing us to engage in activities such as sports, hobbies, travel, and simply enjoying time with our children or grandchildren.

The essence of maintaining good health lies in its ability to enable us to do the things we love and explore new places. However, neglecting our health can lead to limitations that restrict our ability to enjoy life to its fullest. The consequence of letting our health deteriorate is profound, raising the question of the true value of our efforts if we are unable to enjoy the fruits of our labor due to health constraints.

> ***It is crucial to prioritize our health and work on maintaining it consistently rather than postponing it until a more convenient time.***

Stress and neglect can lead to a decline in health, making it increasingly difficult to regain it once lost. Therefore, it's imperative to recognize the importance of health and place it at the forefront of our priorities.

Waiting until it's "too late" is not an option. Health must be seen as a critical element of our lives, deserving of our attention and care. By doing so, we ensure that we can lead active, fulfilling lives without the limitations imposed by poor health.

Freedom of Purpose

At the very top of what I consider important in life is finding one's purpose, understanding the significance of our actions, and the impact we wish to leave on others.

This realization, however, didn't dawn on me until much later in my journey. During my younger years, while I was deeply engrossed in my business and professional endeavors, these considerations of deeper meaning were not at the forefront of my mind.

What I've come to understand is that beyond the years of heavy involvement in our careers, there exists a need to remain relevant and engaged. The desire to maintain a purposeful existence becomes a key driver.

> **Once financial stability is achieved, the absence of a deeper, guiding purpose can leave one feeling adrift.**

It's the sense of purpose, the people we aim to support, and the missions we wish to embark on that provide the motivation to wake up every morning with enthusiasm. In my view, even when one is younger and caught up in the "busyness" of family and career, it's essential to spare thought for these deeper questions of legacy and impact.

I've had the opportunity to remind our members to consider their long-term influence and purpose, ensuring such reflections are not postponed until retirement or the sale of a business.

Discovering and focusing on this fifth level of freedom—the pursuit of impact, significance, purpose, and meaning—is crucial and not something to be deferred. It's a very important aspect of life that we all need to think about and weave into the fabric of our daily existence to avoid feeling lost when our primary professional commitments end.

Becoming Your Own Financial Advocate

I'm not giving you personal, specific advice here because I don't know your personal situation. Until you understand the variables at play in the economy and in your life, you are just rolling the dice.

If you have no game plan, you're rolling the dice. That's why becoming your own financial advocate is vital—educating yourself, and taking input from experts in order to make **your own decisions** regarding your financial future.

I've seen too many plans gone wrong. Plans made by well-meaning financial advisors and financial planners who are still playing the accumulation game with their clients because that is all they know how to do.

The accumulation game is what is promoted and given to you on Wall Street. It is where you put your money in stocks or bonds. Where they recommend the 60-40 portfolio. It has been the standard for many years.

It's a model that is outdated and no longer makes any sense in this economy.

So why do they continue using the accumulation model if it doesn't work?

Because it's safe . . . for them. As long as financial advisors follow the "Rules of Wall Street" then even when the market tanks and you lose capital (this happens through every downturn and major shift in the market cycle) they are protected.

"REMEMBER, JOEY, LIFE IS A GOOD PREPARATION FOR STOCKS-- LOTS OF UPS AND DOWNS."

They don't get in trouble. And, they still get paid. This is just part of the accumulation game. If you don't want to go through that, you will have to put in some work to find a different way. Especially in the face of the major market correction we're just beginning to confront.

The Fastest Path to Freedom and Autonomy

There are no freebies. There is no bright and shiny object that will be the end all. There is no magic bullet that will save us all. Even blindly throwing money into real estate investments is not the answer.

There are only two ways that will leave you with the knowledge and acumen to be prepared for every downturn, to create wealth and keep it.

The first one is to do the work as I did for 20 plus years. I created my own network and honed my skills and abilities to acquire and create Plan B assets in real estate.

If you are younger, that's a great way to get started. If you are older and you don't want to waste time, then that leaves the second option. You need to collapse time. Fold time by gaining access to a group or network that will help you learn faster and find ways to protect your investments and build wealth.

> **Fold time by gaining access to a group or network that will help you learn faster and find ways to protect your investments and build wealth.**

That's what we do in Freedom Founders. It may not be something that's right for you. And that's okay. I still want to share this message because there's no time like today to start figuring out your game plan for tomorrow.

This Economy Will Fall. Will You Fall with It?

Today's economy, held up by stilts, is ready to collapse with the first wave of the tide rushing in. This approaching storm will blow it over, but it's up to you to decide whether you are knocked over with it.

Where are you financially? Do you have any safety measures or hedge positions to protect your wealth?

It's a travesty to see people who have worked hard all their life, accomplished society's definition of success, and put money away wherever they were told to put it . . . Only to see, as they approach the end of what should have been a good long career, 50% of their nest egg washed away by the economic downturns.

They are left confused at what happened while their financial advisor says to "ride it out" because they can only recommend what they know. If your capital is all tied to the financial markets, you will get beat up with it.

No Room for Error—Final Warning

Now is the time to get educated and make a change. It does not matter where you are in your life. You may be younger with more time, or not. Either way, economic headwinds are heading for us all. And there won't be as much leeway like we've had in the past forty years with the lowering cost of capital.

If you are mid career, you may be nearing a large inflection point that can determine the state of your financial future. This means you need to guard against taking any large hit to your capital right now.

If you are towards the end of your career and wanting to sell the business or practice, you need to learn where to put your capital before selling. If you are no longer working your equity in your business, you will be completely at the whims and mercy of the market. If you have never studied how the market behaves and shifts before, you may be in store for a lot of frustration, maybe even desperation.

Don't let that be you.

AFTERWORD: WHAT IS FREEDOM FOUNDERS?

Freedom Founders evolved organically from my own experiences creating personal financial freedom in my early 40s. In the years that followed my practice sale, colleagues began privately confiding with me, wanting to know how I was able to exit practice mid-career without financial constraint. I began to guide and teach some of the frameworks I had learned through my own experience.

Fast forward to today, Freedom Founders has become my "Next" and my primary avenue of creating impact and significance. This is a group and community of high-income professionals who are working together to achieve financial security, passive income, and diversified wealth through strategic real estate investments, tax-efficient wealth-building strategies, and collaborative networking opportunities.

It is a place for personal transformation—home for the misfits who refuse to buy into the conventional life model offered by society and sold by most financial advisors.

We curate real estate investments better than any other group that I am aware of, but what many find when they become a part of the community is that real estate is only a vehicle by which one can create the life you truly desire.

With the right frameworks, investing is the easy part. The real challenge comes from embracing freedom in each area of one's life and finding the permission and the courage to build the life you really want.

DIY vs. Done "With" You.

Most real estate groups and education out there is geared towards one of two outcomes:

1. Making You a Landlord.

They send you out into your local neighborhood to find deals, orchestrate the project, dealing with contractors, tenants . . . I call this becoming an "accidental landlord."

This could be a viable path for a young person with more time than money (it is the path that I took before I had a practice or a family). But at a certain point in your career, you begin to desire a path that does not require starting from scratch or reinventing the wheel. Is it possible to fold time and climb on the shoulders of those who have gone before?

2. Selling You Specific Deals.

The reality is that most real estate groups are commission-based and designed to sell investors into specific deals in which the group facilitators are often

GPs (General Partners in the deal) and stand to profit significantly from selling their own projects.

> **Freedom Founders does not sell real estate. We are high level connectors, educators and guides.**

Through our reputation and my decades of experience, I curate and bring together a network of relationships that provide access points to investment opportunities in a variety of real estate asset classes. I do not have any financial interest in where our members choose to invest.

It's All About Community!

1. Community and Mentorship.

Freedom Founders offers a supportive community and mentorship network specifically designed for high-income practitioners. The community provides a space for like-minded individuals to collaborate, share experiences, and gain insights and guidance on wealth creation and passive income strategies.

2. Financial Independence and Wealth Building.

The community is centered around the pursuit of financial independence and achieving sustainable wealth through strategic investments. We aim to empower members to take control of their financial futures and leverage their professional success to build diversified income streams, particularly through real estate.

3. Education and Resources.

We provide members with access to educational resources, proprietary content, and expert guidance in real estate investing, tax-efficient wealth building, asset protection, and legacy planning. The community offers a wealth of knowledge and insights tailored to the unique financial situations and career paths of high-income professionals.

4. Strategic Real Estate Investing.

Real estate investing is a cornerstone of our wealth-building philosophy. We guide members through learning about passive income generation, cash flow optimization, leveraging tax advantages, and diversifying real estate portfolios to create long-term wealth.

5. Legacy Planning and Asset Protection.

We also address elements of legacy planning, asset preservation, and risk management in long-term wealth building. Members gain access to guidance on estate planning, asset protection, and succession planning to safeguard and transfer generational wealth.

The Freedom Founders Community serves as a comprehensive platform that equips high-income professionals with the knowledge, resources, and support needed to pursue financial independence, build sustainable wealth, and create passive income streams.

Through our focus on real estate investing, tax-efficient strategies, and community engagement, we give our members a pathway to achieve long-term financial security and fulfillment.

Ready to Learn More?

Whenever you're ready, here are additional resources and ways I can help fast-track you to your journey to freedom of time, money, relationships, health, and purpose.

1. Other Books I've Written That Dive Deeper:

Own Your Freedom: Sustainable Wealth for a Volatile World, by Dr. David Phelps with Dan S. Kennedy, www.OwnYourFreedomBook.com

What's Your Next?: The Blueprint For Creating Your Freedom Lifestyle, by Dr. David Phelps, www.FindYourNext.com

Getting the Band Back Together: How a Band of Renegades Rediscovered Their Lives and Gained Total Financial & Time Freedom in Less Than 36 Months, by Dr. David Phelps www.RediscoveringYourLife.com

The Apprentice Model: A Young Leader's Guide to an Anti-Traditional Life, by Dr. David Phelps, www.ApprenticeModelBook.com

Inflation: The Silent Retirement Killer, by Dr. David Phelps, www.InflationBook.com

From High Income To High Net Worth: Alternative Investment Strategies to Stop Trading Time for Dollars and Start Creating True Freedom by Dr. David Phelps, www.HighIncomeBook.com

2. Get Your Retirement Scorecard:

Benchmark your retirement and wealth-building against hundreds of other practice professionals and business owners. Get personalized feedback on your biggest opportunities and leverage points. Go to www.FreedomFounders.com/Scorecard to take the three-minute assessment and get your scorecard.

3. **Listen to My Podcast:**

    I post weekly interviews and monologues that explore the topics of this book and more—how practitioners can become their own financial advocate amidst today's economic volatility and uncertainty. Listen in at: www.DentistFreedomBlueprint.com

4. **Schedule a Call with My Team:**

    If you'd like to replace your active income with passive investment income within two to three years, and you have at least $1 million in available capital (can include residential or practice equity, business equity, whole life insurance and retirement accounts), then visit the following link to schedule a call with my team. They can help explore potential alignment and help you discover your pathway to freedom: www.FreedomFounders.com/Discover.

Thank you for reading, and I look forward to helping you achieve Financial Freedom!

Dr. David Phelps, DDS

ABOUT THE AUTHOR: DR. DAVID PHELPS

Who Is Dr. David Phelps?

And Why Should You Listen to Him about YOUR Money?

A Practice Owner Turned CEO and Leader

David owned and managed a private practice dental office for over twenty-one years before his daughter's health crisis served as a dramatic wake-up call in his life. David's "Plan B" (a portfolio of cash-flow producing real estate assets) gave him the Freedom to sell his practice mid-career and focus 100% on what matters most to him.

David is a renegade, he does not follow the majority but lives life and does business on his own terms and is not dictated to by others.

America's #1 Authority on Creating Freedom in Life and Business

David is the author of 6 published business, finance and success books. As a nationally recognized keynote speaker, David brings dynamic energy and rare insights into how to create financial freedom through passive income, how to build a real business that doesn't take over your life, anti-traditional real estate investing, private lending, wealth-building legacy, and how to take responsibility and "own" your life.

A Leader Born Through Crisis

Sitting with his daughter in the hospital room after her battle with leukemia and a life-saving liver transplant, Dr. David Phelps realized what matters most. It was not his career as a dentist that had consumed his daily life for over twenty-one years. He needed to be present for his daughter Jenna.

He decided he would no longer practice dentistry. Instead, he developed his "Plan B."

He drew inspiration from his years of investing avidly in real estate that began in dental school with a joint-venture with his father. By leveraging the lessons and capital he had acquired, David built an investment portfolio that could generate enough passive income to leave his dental practice and be the father his daughter needed.

Escaping Trading Time for Dollars

David's radical new life intrigued his peers, who asked him how they too could command control of their wealth and time. By bringing together his two worlds—high-income medical professionals and real estate professionals—David created a powerful network of like-minded professionals who could support each other on their own paths to financial and personal freedom.

He called this group Freedom Founders, and as its leader he found his purpose: helping his colleagues break the chains of enslavement to their practices and financial fears and create freedom in their lives.

With his own life as proof, David challenges the traditional model of wealth building, which preaches abdicating control over one's money to advisors and entrusting all of one's investing capital to Wall Street.

David has witnessed too many high income professionals blindly trust the traditional path only to have their hard-earned wealth wiped out by the volatility of the public market. Through Freedom Founders, David exhorts his members to **take back control** of their investing capital from their practices and 401(k) plans, **put it to work** in more stable, capital producing assets like real estate, and **always stay focused on their freedom**.

Your Network Is Your Net Worth

Freedom Founders Mastermind Group began as a meeting of sixteen people over a decade ago and has grown into a community of over one hundred forty members and Service Providers, where his insights into the financial markets, alternative investing, as well as achieving success and fulfillment in life bring members from across the country.

Speaking from his own experience, David strives to instill in his members the courage to lead lives unhindered by the expectations of others and driven by purpose. Following in his footsteps, Freedom Founders members attain the tools to become Free for Life: they can live entirely on the passive income from their real estate investments.

A Recognized Leader in Dentistry and Real Estate

David has been featured in Advantage Forbes Books, The Profitable Dentist, Dental Success Today, The Progressive Orthodontist. He has been awarded the GKIC Marketer of the Year.

David regularly collaborates with countless industry leaders including Dr. Dustin Burleson, Dr. David Maloley, Steven J. Anderson, Scott Manning, Alastair Macdonald, Dr. Scott Leune, Dr. Annisa Holmes, Dr. Christopher Phelps, and many others.

At his own events, he has shared the stage with Garrett Gunderson, Chuck Blakeman, Adam Witty, Tony Rubleski, Thomas Blackwell, and others.

An Expert in the World of Real Estate

David's expertise in the world of real estate includes everything from multi-family apartments, self-storage, commercial properties, retail properties, single-family rentals, structured notes, private debt, managed funds and more. He has successfully weathered multiple market corrections—notably using the 2006–2008 downturn to successfully more than double his net worth.

He is regularly consulted in the creation and management of large multi-investor syndications and funds secured by real estate assets.

Printed in the USA
CPSIA information can be obtained
at www.ICGtesting.com
LVHW020548281024
794667LV00005B/27